The Golden Ratio Cookbook

Copyright 2017, Jen Golbeck
ISBN 978-1-387-40628-9

Table of Contents

TABLE OF CONTENTS..2

NOTES FOR NEW COOKS...5

ABBREVIATIONS...6
MEASUREMENTS AND EQUIVALENTS...6
FOR THE NON-AMERICANS...7
COMMON TEMPERATURES..7
VOLUMES AND WEIGHTS..7
TIPS, TECHNIQUES, AND GADGETS...7

BREAKFAST...11

WAFFLE...12
HOMEMADE EGG MCMUFFINS...12

BREADS..15

CORNBREAD...16
CRANBERRY ORANGE BREAD...16
PUMPKIN BREAD...17
GARLIC BREAD..17

VEGGIES AND POTATOES..19

STEAMED BROCCOLI (AND OTHER VEGGIES)...20
ROASTED BRUSSELS SPROUTS (AND OTHER VEGGIES)..20
SALT POTATOES..21
GARLIC MASHED POTATOES...22

MEALS..24

BROCCOLI APPLE SALAD..25
APPLE FENNEL MANCHEGO SALAD...25

Rainbow Mexican Salad 26
Macaroni and Cheese 27
Fettuccine Alfredo 28

SNACKS 30
Queso Dip 31
Pumpkin Seeds 31

DRINKS 33
Gumby Slumber 34
Classic Margarita 34
Mojito 35
Southside 35
Simple Syrup 35

DESSERTS 37
Graham Cracker Crust 38
Key Lime Pie 38
Whipped Cream 38
Apple Pie 39
Pumpkin Pie 40
Brownies 40
Peanut Butter Cookies 41

DOG TREATS 43
Carrots 44
Peanut Butter Dog Biscuits 44
Dog Birthday Cake 44
Bland Meal 45

FOODS TO WORRY ABOUT 47

Notes for New Cooks

A lot of you who are fans of the Golden Ratio are new cooks, which is great! These recipes are all pretty easy and doable without any fancy ingredients. They are also the things I make most in every day life – a lot of them I make so often that I don't look at recipes anymore.

There are some standard abbreviations and measurements I use here that you may not know if you aren't an experienced cook. This section introduces some of those.

Abbreviations

c -   cup
t -   teaspoon
T -   tablespoon
oz -   ounce
lb -   pound

Measurements and Equivalents

Being able to convert between measurements gets easier with practice. Here are a few basic conversions.

1 Tablespoon = 3 teaspoons
1 Tablespoon = 0.5 oz

1 cup = 16 Tablespoons
1 cup = 8 oz

1 shot = 1.5 oz = 3 Tablespoons (usually, though some people pour 2 oz. shots. Be wary of these people!)

1 stick of butter = ½ cup of butter = ¼ lb of butter

A note on ounces (oz). There are fluid ounces and weight ounces because we Americans like to make things complicated. Fluid ounces measure volume and are used to measure liquids. A cup is 8 oz. One ounce is 2 Tablespoons. I will usually stick to teaspoons and tablespoons and cups, but you may run into other recipes that use ounces. Notably, drink recipes commonly use ounces.

Also, non-American types use weights (usually grams) instead of cups for things like flour and such. It's so confusing. Honestly, I end up just using a Google search to convert it. You can say "Convert 100 grams of flour to cups" and it will do it for you!

For the Non-Americans

Sorry we have such weird systems. Here are some conversions for you.

Common Temperatures

All the temperatures I give here are in Fahrenheit. Here are common temps and their Celsius conversions:

300° F = 150 C
350° F = 175 C
375° F = 190 C
400° F = 200 C
425° F = 220 C
450° F = 225 C

Volumes and Weights

Here are some rough approximations for converting my measurements to yours.

1 oz = 28 g (but only in weight ounces, not fluid ounces)
1 oz = 30 ml (the liquid kind of ounce)
1 teaspoon = 5 ml
1 Tablespoon = 15 ml
1 c = 250 ml
1 pound = 0.45 kilograms

Tips, Techniques, and Gadgets

Most of these recipes can be made without any special equipment or fancy techniques. As you start cooking more, it's a good excuse to learn a few new skills or to pick up a few things for the kitchen. Most of the tools I mention – a garlic press, dicer, and steamer basket – are pretty cheap and will make your cooking life so much happier. If you get serious, it's totally worth investing in a food processor and a stand mixer. I use mine 4-5 times a week, but they are a bit of a bigger investment.

We've put up a page with all the cooking equipment in the Golden Ratio household, so if you want to add to your kitchen, you can see what we use. It's all at thegoldenratio.dog/store. You'll see I usually buy budget items for common cooking gadgets. They work just fine!

Here are a few techniques, tips, and details on gadgets that may help if you're just starting. It's a random list of stuff I have thought of as I've been putting these recipes together.

Soften butter by microwaving it for 8 seconds (your microwave may vary, and it takes like 1 second to go from soft to melted, so practice). It's good to soften it before baking, so it incorporates better with the other ingredients. If a recipe calls for softened butter, don't use *melted* butter. It will make whatever you're baking come out flat. There's some really interesting chemistry in how butter combines with other ingredients.

Salt – learning to salt things properly is not a trivial skill, but it's SO important. Many dishes will be super bland when they are done unless you add enough salt. Salt doesn't just make stuff taste salty; it amplifies flavors (which is why you see salt in recipes for cookies and brownies and such). Of course, if you add too much, you ruin it. The best way to learn to salt enough is to add a bit at a time, taste, and add more over and over. The more you cook, the better sense you get for how much to start with so the process speeds up. Any savory recipe you read requires salt and pepper to taste at the end (even if the recipe doesn't say that), so don't skimp! (I grew up with a mom who was a dietitian and we never ate much salt and it was a revelation to me when I moved out and learned to cook on my own that things could be so much better with the right amount!)

Testing for doneness in cakes and breads is usually done by sticking a toothpick in. You should stab it right in the middle and it should come out clean. If there's a crumb clinging to it, that's ok, but there shouldn't be any damp batter on it. If it has batter, bake for another 5 minutes or so and check again (poke in a different spot). All ovens are different, so don't be surprised if your recipe cooks much faster or slower than what a recipe says.

Get a dicer! This is a little device with a metal grid over a box. You put something like an onion on the grid, push the lid down, and it pushes the onion through the grid into the box where it comes out in perfectly diced little bits. My mom once got me one of these as a sort of joke gift, and I use it basically every time I cook. Sure, you can totally dice onions and peppers with a knife, but this is so fast and consistent. It's probably the kitchen gadget I use most and is *so* worth the $10

Bake vs. Broil on your oven - Most ovens have a top and bottom heating element. The normal mode of using the oven (called "bake" on most) will turn those both on and you can pick the temperature. Broil, on the other hand, only turns on the top element and it usually turns it on high. This will quickly brown something under it and is also the best way to make nachos. You can control how fast the broiler gets to the food by changing the rack the food is on. If you want to say, quickly brown the top of a lasagna that's already cooked, put it on the top rack. If you're making nachos, put the cheese and stuff on your chips, and put them on the middle rack with the broiler on. That keeps them far enough from the heat that everything will warm up, but it will melt the cheese fast and get it ready before the chips have a chance to get soggy or soft.

Potatoes – there are different types of potatoes. Russet potatoes are the ones you normally have when you eat baked potatoes and they are great for baking. Yukon Gold and red potatoes work better for making mashed potatoes; if you try to mash russet potatoes, they get sort of grainy. A good guide is that if the skin of the potato is a little waxy looking, it will make good mashed potatoes. Sweet potatoes are a whole other thing, and they are good baked or mashed or roasted.

Breakfast

Waffle

2 c flour
2 c water
2 eggs
4 t baking powder
1 t cinnamon (optional)
1 T honey (optional)
1 t vanilla (optional)

Beat eggs and water until the eggs are well mixed. Add in flour, baking powder, and any flavorings until batter is smooth. Don't over-mix or the waffles will be tough! Spray your waffle iron well with Pam or other cooking spray so they don't stick. Our regular sized waffle iron uses about 1 cup of batter per waffle.

Serve straight up to dogs, or with toppings for humans.

Homemade Egg McMuffins

1 English muffin
1 egg
1 slice of cheese

Split and toast the English muffin. For the egg, if you have a big round cookie cutter or biscuit ring, put that in a frying pan. Heat pan to medium-high. Spray the inside of the ring with cooking spray. Beat the egg and add it to the inside of the ring. Mix it up a bit. Once the egg is firm enough that you can flip it, gently remove the ring and flip the egg. If you don't have a ring, you can crack your egg directly into the pan and fry it or scramble the eggs and mold them into a neat pile before they set, then flip the pile to get something close to a molded ring.

If you have an oven with a broiler, put the cheese on the muffin and broil it for a minute to melt the cheese. If not, you can add the cheese to the top of the eggs right after you flip them and melt it for a minute while the eggs finish cooking. Add the eggs to the English muffin and you're done!

Breads

Cornbread

1 c cornmeal
1 c flour
½ c sugar
1 T baking powder

½ t salt
1 c milk
1 large egg
¼ c melted butter

Preheat the oven to 400.

Combine butter, egg, and milk and stir until well blended. Add all the rest of the ingredients and stir until they are just wet – don't over-mix or it will get tough. It's ok if the batter is a little lumpy. Pour into a cake pan or 8x8 baking dish sprayed well with cooking spray. Bake for 20-25 minutes until the top is golden brown.

Serve with butter or honey.

Cranberry Orange Bread

This is a really good treat to make for potlucks and other holiday gatherings because it has the flavors people expect but is different than most dishes.

2 c. flour
1 c. sugar
1.5 t. baking powder
1 t. salt
1/2 t baking soda

3/4 c. orange juice
1 egg.
2 T softened butter
1.5 c whole cranberries
1/2 c. walnut

Preheat the oven to 350 degrees. In a bowl, mix the dry ingredients. Add juice, egg, and butter to the dry stuff and mix until you have a good batter. Stir in cranberries and walnuts. Don't worry if your cranberries are frozen – they will work fine. Spray or butter a loaf pan. Spread the batter evenly into the pan and bake for 55 minutes. Cool in pan for 10 minutes and then transfer to a rack to cool.

Pumpkin Bread

I confess I once ate an entire loaf of this bread over the course of the day after I ran a marathon. Yay carbs!

1 ½ c flour
½ t baking powder
¾ t baking soda
¼ t salt
½ t ground ginger
¼ t nutmeg

1 T ground cinnamon
1 stick of butter (½ c)
½ c firmly packed dark brown sugar
1 c white sugar
3 eggs
1 c pumpkin puree

Preheat the oven to 350 and grease a loaf pan.

Cream the butter and sugars together until they are white and fluffy. Add the eggs and pumpkin and mix for 2-3 minutes. Then add in all the dry ingredients and mix it all up until you have a smooth batter.

Pour the batter into the prepared pan and bake at 350 until a toothpick inserted into the center comes out clean, about 55 minutes. Transfer the pan to a wire rack and let cool for 15 minutes.

Garlic Bread

1 baguette
2 T softened butter
2 T olive oil
1 t garlic powder

1 t dried parsley
2 cloves crushed garlic
2 T grated parmesan cheese

Preheat your oven to 350. Slice the baguette into thin slices, about ½ inch thick, but don't cut quite all the way through. You want the loaf to be connected at the bottom. In a bowl, mix all the other ingredients into a saucy, garlicky, amazing paste. Using a spatula or brush, spread each slice of the baguette with garlic butter. Wrap the loaf in aluminum foil with the fold at the top. Bake for about 15 minutes, then, open the foil at the top and bake another 5-10 minutes until the top is crispy. Serve immediately!

Veggies and Potatoes

Steamed Broccoli (and other veggies)

In a pot that's big enough to hold an inch of water, some kind of separator, and all your broccoli, add about an inch of water and put it on high to boil. Meanwhile, cut off the thick stems of the broccoli and break the rest into little florets. (Note: you can slice the stems into thin pieces if you want to eat them or give them to your dog – Maggie loves the stems!)

Put in some kind of separator to keep the water away from the broccoli. I use a steaming basket, which you can get for cheap online or in any home store. But you can use a colander or a cooling rack or anything that fits in your pan.

Put that into the boiling water and put your broccoli on top of that. Cover and steam until the broccoli is soft enough to be pierced by a fork. Don't overcook it! If it gets olive green colored or turns mushy, you've gone too long.

Note that this technique works for steaming lots of veggies – cauliflower, sliced carrots, green beans, and more.

Roasted Brussels Sprouts (and other veggies)

Preheat your oven to 425. Slice off the tough bottom of your Brussels sprouts and then slice each sprout in half (or quarters if you have giant ones, but smaller ones always taste better). Remove any brown leaves and slice off any brown spots.

Add the Brussels sprouts to a cookie sheet. Drizzle with olive oil. You'll use about 1-2 T, but you'll get the hang of it as you make them often and you won't have to measure. The goal is to use enough oil so that, after you toss them around, there's just a super light coating of oil on each sprout. They should glisten! Sprinkle with salt and pepper to taste. I like a lot of salt. Mix it all together good with your hands so the sprouts are thoroughly covered.

Roast until they are just starting to brown. Any single leaves on the sheet will be dark brown. The sprouts should pierce easily with a fork but the should not be mushy.

These are good served as is or with a squeeze of lemon juice or a sprinkle of parmesan cheese.

Note this technique works well for lots of other veggies – asparagus, broccoli, cauliflower, potatoes (sweet and regular), onions, carrots. You just have to change how long you cook them. The stab-it-with-a-fork-test is a good way to check if they are done.

Salt Potatoes

1 pound of tiny potatoes
½ c salt
8-12 cups of water (enough to cover your potatoes by a couple inches in the pot)

This dish comes from Syracuse, so you're learning a local specialty here! Add the salt to the water and bring it to a boil. Yes, it's a *lot* of salt. **Do not cut the potatoes!** This only works because you have whole, tiny potatoes. Once the water is boiling, add the potatoes and cook until they are easy to pierce with a fork, about 10 minutes. Drain them in a colander but don't rinse them. They will form a salty crust as the water evaporates. Serve them immediately either drizzled with melted butter or with small dishes of melted butter that you can dip them in.

Garlic Mashed Potatoes

1 pound of Yukon Gold or red potatoes
2 cloves crushed garlic
½ c butter
1/3 c milk (or half and half)
½ t steak seasoning
½ t garlic powder
salt

Fill a large pot half full with water and bring it to a boil. If you like your potatoes pealed, this is the time to do it. I like the peel just fine in my mashed potatoes. Dice the potatoes into cubes about 1 inch square, but don't be too particular about this. Just make sure they are all the same size. Add the potatoes to the boiling water and cook until they can be easily smushed with a fork.

Drain the potatoes and return them to the pot with no heat. Add all the other ingredients and mash until they reach the right level of creaminess. If they seem a bit dry, add a little more milk, about 2 tablespoons at a time, and then mash some more. Add salt. Start with about 1 teaspoon but add as much as you need for them to taste great. You can also add more steak seasoning or garlic powder if you like, too.

For a healthier version, you can use less butter. I usually use about 2 tablespoons when I make this for a normal dinner.

Meals

Broccoli Apple Salad

For the salad
4 cups of broccoli florets
2 apples
1 c chopped walnuts
1 c diced carrots
½ c raisins
¼ of a red onion, diced

For the dressing
1 c Greek yogurt
2 T apple cider vinegar
3 T honey

The key to this salad is to cut everything into small, bite-sized bits. That means chopping up your broccoli and apples smaller than you might otherwise. Once you have diced all your veggies, mix the dressing in a separate bowl. If you want it more decadent, switch out part of the yogurt with mayonnaise. Mix it all together if you're going to eat it all at once. Otherwise, use some dressing on the salad you're going to eat, and store the two parts separate in the fridge so they will keep longer. This recipe is adapted from *Cooking Classy*'s recipe.

Apple Fennel Manchego Salad

My version of a Jaleo classic. If you come to Washington, DC, eat there for mind-blowingly good tapas!

For the salad
1 apple
¼ lb manchego cheese
1 whole fennel

For the dressing
2 T olive oil
3 T apple cider vinegar
salt to taste

Thinly slice the fennel. If you have a mandoline, use that (and watch your fingers – from painful experience, I would recommend using a mesh glove!). Dice the apple and manchego into small, bite-sized pieces of whatever shape you like. Mix all the salad parts together

To make the dressing, combine the ingredients and either shake them in a jar (my preferred method), or whisk them in a bowl until they are well combined. Add as much dressing to the salad as you like and enjoy!

Rainbow Mexican Salad

For the salad
1.5 pounds sweet potatoes
1 can (or 1.5 c) black beans
1 red bell pepper
½ a red onion
½ bunch of cilantro
1 can (or 1.5 c) corn

For the lime crema
1 c greek yogurt or sour cream
Zest and juice of 1 lime
1 clove of crushed garlic
¼ t salt

To roast the sweet potatoes, preheat the oven to 400. Cut the potatoes into bite sized chunks. Drizzle with olive oil and add salt and, if you like, a little cumin. Toss that well so the potatoes are evenly coated. Roast for about 30 minutes until they are soft.

Drain and rinse the corn and black beans if you are using them from a can. Dice the red onion and red pepper into very small bits. Slice the leaves off the cilantro bunch and roughly chop it. Combine all the veggies in a bowl and mix well.

For the lime crema, mix all ingredients in a separate bowl. This stuff is delicious and you can use it on tacos, nachos, burritos, quesadillas, and all other kinds of Mexican foods.

If you're serving the whole dish, mix it all together. If you want to serve a bit at a time, use just the crema you need for your serving and store the veggies and crema separately in the fridge.

This recipe was adapted from *Budget Bytes's* Roasted Sweet Potato Rainbow Salad.

Macaroni and Cheese

You can substitute the same amount of any type of cheese and substitute any veggie (or just leave the veg out entirely).

8 ounces of pasta (macaroni, penne, etc.)
1¼ c milk
2 T butter
2 T flour
Preheat the oven to 375

1/8 t. cayenne pepper (optional)
4 oz cheese (I like smoked gouda)
1 bag of fresh spinach (or 1 cup of any veggies)
1/2 c bread crumbs

Cook the noodles until al dente.

In a saucepan, melt the butter over medium heat and stir in flour until it's bubbly. Slowly stir in the milk a little at a time and keep stirring until it starts to thicken. (Note: you now have the base for tons of different sauces!) Add the cayenne, salt & pepper to taste, and bring it all to a boil for a couple minutes. Add the cheese and stir until it's melted. If you're adding veggies, add them now (for spinach, it will seem like a lot, but don't worry - it will wilt really quickly in the cheese sauce and become smol...).

Meanwhile, make bread crumbs by chopping up some stale bread in a blender or food processor and seasoning with parmesan cheese, salt, pepper, garlic powder, or anything else you like until they taste good. You can, of course, just buy breadcrumbs at the store, too.

Spray a casserole dish with non-stick spray. Add the noodles, pour the sauce over them, and stir. Top with the bread crumbs. Bake for about 20 minutes until it's golden brown and bubbly.

Fettuccine Alfredo

1 pound of fettuccine
1 cup heavy cream
1 stick of butter (1/2 a cup)

¾ c grated parmesan cheese
2 T parsley

This is a ridiculously rich and decadent dish. Do not eat this every night or you will get fat and/or sick. But if you have a date coming over? This will impress!

Cook the fettuccini according to the package instructions. Get yourself some fresh pasta if you want this to be extra special. In a saucepan, heat the cream and butter over medium-low heat. You don't want it to boil or it will burn and separate. Just get it really hot until there are tiny bubbles. Once the butter is melted and the cream is hot, stir in the cheese and stir/whisk with intensity until it's incorporated. You should have a nice, smooth sauce. Add the parsley. Serve over the pasta. If you want to pretend this is healthy, it's really good with some steamed broccoli.

Snacks

Queso Dip

1 pound yellow American cheese
1 can of Rotel
8 oz beer (about 2/3rds of a bottle)

Drain the Rotel and add it, and the beer, to a sauce pan over medium-high heat. Cut the cheese up into cubes or tear it into small bits. The smaller your cheese pieces, the faster this will be ready. Let the whole mess heat up until it's simmering. Then, start stirring. It's ready when there are no chunks of cheese left, and you have just smooth, golden goodness. Serve with Tostitos Scoops (or any chips, but scoops are the best).

Note: you are hereby warned that other kinds of cheese don't work as well as American. They will separate or get clumpy. You can try it, but yellow American is the best. You will do best to get it from the deli, too. Don't use Kraft slices. Deli cheese costs about the same but it tastes better and is easier to work with.

This is also a great cheese sauce to put on a burger. We make one called the El Jefe that has this cheese, guacamole, and Doritos on top. It's *amazing*.

Pumpkin Seeds

Take the pumpkin seeds from your pumpkin and separate them from the flesh. There's no fast or easy way to do this. Usually, you get a ton of seeds in a pumpkin, so don't worry about getting every last one.

Preheat your oven to 300. Rinse the seeds and drain them but don't dry them, or they might stick together. Oil a cookie sheet with olive oil or cooking spray and spread a single layer of seeds on the sheet. Bake at 300 until they are dry and getting slightly golden, about 30 minutes. Take them out, add a drizzle of olive oil and whatever seasonings you like. I usually just do salt, but you can be as creative! Try Old Bay, garlic, paprika, taco seasoning, ranch dressing mix, cinnamon, pumpkin spice (but please don't try all of those together).

Drinks

Gumby Slumber

This is the signature cocktail of Little Palm Island Resort, where the Golden Ratio's mom & dad got married. It's tropical and delicious!

1.5 oz Captain Morgan rum
1.5 oz coconut rum
1.5 oz orange juice

1 oz pineapple juice
a dash of cranberry juice

Pour all the ingredients over ice, stir, and serve. For an authentic finish, add a pinch of coconut that's been soaked in 151 rum.

You can make this stronger by using 2 oz shots, but be warned – that can give you a headache right quick. I often make this weaker by using ¾ oz pours (basically, half a shot) of each rum. It's good however you do it.

Classic Margarita

Never use a margarita mix. The classic is so good and so easy!

1.5 oz silver tequila (the better your tequila, the better you will feel tomorrow)
1 oz Cointreau or other orange liqueur
1 oz lime juice (fresh squeezed is best)

Put it all in a shaker with ice and shake until the outside gets frosty. Give it a taste – some people like sweeter margaritas and you can add a little simple syrup if you'd like it sweeter. Don't go overboard! Just add about 1 teaspoon at a time, shake it a couple times to mix it in, and taste again.

If you want salted rims on your glass, rub a slice of lime on the rim (or use water in a pinch). Put a thin layer of salt on a plate and stick your damp glass rim in the salt and swirl it around. Give the salt a few seconds to dry on there. (Note: this technique also works with sugar if you ever want a sugared rim). Serve over ice in the glass.

Mojito

I have made lots of mojitos in my day, but we recently discovered Pyrat rum and it is maybe the most delicious thing ever. If you are a rum lover, go find this and use it in your mojitos and thank me later.

2 oz rum
1 oz simple syrup (recipe below)
3 lime wedges
7 mint leaves (give or take)

Put the mint, simple syrup, and limes in the bottom of a glass. Muddle them – this basically means smash them with something (preferably a muddler, but use what you have). Do it about 5-8 times until your mint is slightly crushed, the juice is mostly out of your limes, and you have a big green mess down there. Add the rum, stir, and fill the glass with crushed ice. Top off with a splash of club soda if you like!

Southside

Here's a secret about cocktails. A lot of them are just the same thing with a different liquor or citrus and that makes it a different drink. The southside is basically a mojito but with gin.

2 oz gin (Plymouth is great in this drink)
1 oz simple syrup
1 oz lemon juice
8 mint leaves

In a shaker, put the mint, syrup, and lemon juice in the bottom and muddle. Add the gin and ice and shake gently 5 or 6 times, just to get it cold and well mixed. Strain and serve. Garnish with a mint leaf.

Simple Syrup

This is used in so many cocktails, and it's good to have on hand if you start mixing a lot of drinks. In a mason jar (or whatever you've got), mix 1 part sugar and 1 part hot water (I usually do ½ c of each in a batch). Shake it hard until the sugar dissolves. Store in the fridge.

Desserts

Graham Cracker Crust

Anything you put in this crust will be delicious.

6 graham crackers
¾ c whole almonds
½ c sugar
½ c melted butter

In a food processor, pulse the sugar, crackers, and almonds until you have something uniformly small and crumbly. Add the melted butter and pulse to combine. Press this into a pie pan, up the sides and on the bottom. Bake for 10 minutes at 350.

Key Lime Pie

1 prepared graham cracker crust
1/2 cup lime juice
14. oz can condensed sweetened milk
3 egg yolks

Add juice, milk, and eggs to a blender. Mix well. Pour into crust and bake 15 minutes at 325 to set the pie. Let cool and then refrigerate.

The pie is good alone, but much better with fresh whipped cream.

Whipped Cream

Good for key lime pie and pretty much anything else.

½ c heavy cream   **2 T powdered sugar**

Add the cream to a bowl and beat it on high speed until it forms peaks. Don't beat it too long or it will turn into butter!

Apple Pie

This is my great grandmother's pie recipe. True story: when I met the Golden Ratio's dad I made him this pie. He loved it and I have made him a pie every week for the last 6 years and counting because pie = love.

For the pie filling
6 apples
½ c sugar
2 T flour
1 T cinnamon

For the topping
½ c butter
½ c flour
½ c sugar

Preheat the oven to 425 F. Cut the apples into chunks or thin slices. Mix well with the sugar, flour, and cinnamon. Heap these into a pie crust. Arrange them so hopefully nothing falls out. It will look super heaped up, but the apples cook down, so don't worry.

For the topping, combine all the ingredients. If you have a stand mixer or food processor, you can combine it that way. If not, cut in the butter with a pastry blender or two knives until mixture is coarse, like cornmeal. Sprinkle this mixture evenly over top of pie and pat it down to keep it in place.

Slide pie into a brown paper grocery bag. Fold the open end under. Put the whole bag in the oven. Bake at 425 for 90 minutes. You might want to place a cookie sheet on a rack under the bag to catch drips. The bag might get a little brown, but I promise it won't catch on fire (but be smart – don't let it touch the heating elements obviously).

Very carefully, remove the bag from the oven. Don't tilt it or the delicious pie juices will spill out. Split the bag open and let the pie cool.

Pumpkin Pie

1 (9 inch) unbaked deep dish pie crust
3/4 cup sugar
1 T cinnamon
1/2 t salt
1 t ground ginger

1/2 t ground cloves
2 eggs
1 (15 oz) can pumpkin (no spices added)
1 (12 fluid oz) can evaporated milk

Preheat the oven to 425 F.

Blend everything together and pour it into the pie shell.

Bake for 15 minutes. Then reduce the temperature to 350 and bake for 40-50 minutes longer until knife inserted near the center comes out clean. Cool on wire rack for 2 hours. I like my pumpkin pie cold, so after cooling, I refrigerate it overnight. As always, it's better with whipped cream!

Brownies

2 eggs
3/4 c sugar
1 t vanilla
1/2 c melted butter

3/4 c Ghirardelli sweet ground chocolate
2/3 c flour
1/4 t baking powder
1/4 t salt

Preheat the oven to 350 F. Mix the eggs and sugar, then add the butter. Mix it up with everything else and bake it for 20-25 minutes. These can vary a lot in how long they take to cook, so be sure you test with a toothpick to make sure they aren't underdone.

Peanut Butter Cookies

1/2 c butter
1/2 c peanut butter
1/2 c sugar
1/2 c brown sugar
1 egg

1/2 t vanilla
1 1/4 c flour
3/4 t baking soda
1/2 t salt

Preheat the oven to 375. Cream together everything except the flour. Then, gently mix in the flour until it is just incorporated (as always with flour, too much mixing makes your baked goods tough). Shape the dough into 1.5-2 inch balls, roll in granulated sugar, place onto cookie sheet, the use a fork to lightly press a crisscross pattern into the cookies and slightly flatten the balls.

Bake 10-12 minutes until the bottoms just barely start to brown. Let cool for 5 minutes on the cookie sheet before transferring them to a cooling rack.

Dog Treats

Carrots

The bigger the better. Serve to dogs raw. See if they backup to take it to their eating spot.

Peanut Butter Dog Biscuits

3 c. flour
1/2 c. oats
2 t baking powder

1-1/2 c. milk
1-1/2 c. peanut butter
2 T. molasses

Mix everything together, kneed slightly, and roll out to 1/2 inch thick. Cut into shapes with a cookie cutter (preferably, bone shaped). Bake at 350 for 20 minutes or until lightly browned. Then, turn off the oven and leave the bones in there until cool. If you're making multiple sheets, take the first ones out after their 20 minutes and then put them back in when it's time to turn the oven off. They will not be sticky and you can stack them if you need the space.

Dog Birthday Cake

1 c finely chopped carrots
1 c flour
1 egg
½ c peanut butter
¼ c vegetable oil
1 t baking soda

This is a birthday cake for your dogs to eat. It's not very sweet and kind of bland by human standards, but you can totally eat some if you want.

Preheat oven to 350. Mix everything together in your food processor or a bowl. Grease a small cake pan and spread this smoothly in the pan. Bake for about 45 minutes until you poke it with a toothpick that comes out clean. Let it cool completely before serving.

Bland Meal

If your dog is feeling bad (vomiting, diarrhea, low appetite) , a bland meal for a few breakfasts / dinners will usually help. This chicken and rice is a great go-to – we keep a few packages of boneless chicken in the freezer just in case someone gets sick. Tip: get the cheapest boneless chicken you can find. You may even find it pre-cut into smaller chunks. Anything will work, but smaller pieces will make it a bit faster and easier to cook.

1.5 pounds of boneless chicken (definitely no bones!)
1 cup white rice (don't use brown or wild – that's tougher on the digestive system)
3-4 cups of water

If your chicken isn't frozen, cut it up into smaller pieces so it cooks faster. Cutting frozen chicken is a pain, so don't bother – it will be fine, but will take a bit longer to cook. Add the chicken, rice, and water to a baking dish and cover with a lid or foil. I bake this at 350 for about 45 minutes to an hour until the chicken isn't pink in the middle.

You can also boil it if you prefer. To do it that way, put it all in a pot, bring that to a boil, and then turn it down to a simmer (medium-low heat) and cook it with the lid on. Add more water if it looks dry partway through cooking. Your dog will love this no matter what, so don't worry about overcooking the chicken or adding too much water. Just be sure the chicken is cooked all the way through and you're good to serve it.

Once it's done cooking, I put this in the food processor for a few pulses to make the chicken bits small (otherwise, the dogs try to eat the chicken and skip the rice). Once your dog smells it, they may want to eat it, but obviously you have to let it cool. I speed that up by smearing about a cup of it on a plate and putting that in the freezer so it cools quickly.

If your dog is vomiting, try giving just a little bit (a few tablespoons) at a time. Let them wait 10-15 minutes after eating and if they keep it down, give a little more.

If your dog has diarrhea, this will help with that. If they don't have diarrhea, you can add some canned pumpkin to what you serve them. That tastes good, soothes the digestive system, and will also help with constipation.

Foods to Worry About

Whenever I post recipes, I usually get a few people asking "can dogs have that?!" (or, since it's the internet, sometimes they just yell at me and tell me I'm killing the girls). Lots of human type food is fine for dogs. Some dogs, like some people, are lactose intolerant (you will smell if this is the case), so they shouldn't have any dairy / cheese. Some dogs have allergies to certain foods. Hopper is really sensitive to certain meats, which isn't a huge problem since our house is vegetarian for humans, but she can't have rawhides or bully sticks. Basically, your dog may vary, but generally, they can eat a lot of human stuff.

However, there are some foods that are really dangerous. Here's a list of some that you should never give your dog:

Alcohol – they react to it way more than we do. Don't give it to them. They could die.

Avocado – it's not a huge problems for dogs in particular, but lots of animals react poorly to them. Stay away to be safe.

Chocolate – I'm sure you know this.

Coffee – the caffeine does bad things to them.

Coconut water – there's a lot of potassium in this that can upset your dog's system

Grapes and Raisins – they can cause kidney failure! And they sneak in to a lot of foods, so be really careful with these.

Macadamia nuts and Walnuts – they don't know why, but these nuts can make dogs vomit, get fevers, or become lethargic.

Onions, Garlic, and Chives – some dogs get stomach upset or gastrointestinal issues from these. Our dogs occasionally eat something we've made with onion or garlic in it and are fine, but you don't want them to eat any of this in large amounts.

Poultry Bones – never let dogs eat bones from birds. They are hollow and splinter and can pierce their stomach or intestine.

Xylitol – this is an artificial sweetener, often found in sugar free candy and gum, and is toxic to dogs.

Yeast – Yeast itself but also raw dough can expand in their stomachs and cause problems.

If your dog gets into something they shouldn't, there are things you can do. One of my previous dogs ate A POUND OF CHOCOLATE COVERED ESPRESSO BEANS. OMG. We caught her in the act! If you catch your dog eating something bad or you know they ate it very recently, you can induce vomiting. Give them about a quarter cup of hydrogen peroxide. They will not want to swallow it and it will make their mouth all foamy. We keep a big syringe at home so we can shoot this down their throat in an emergency (no needle, just a syringe). They should vomit in a few minutes. If not, you can give another quarter cup.

Obviously, call your vet or Animal Poison Control. Poison Control is run by the ASPCA and they are great (I know – I have called many, many times). 888-426-4435. They charge, so call your vet first if they are open.

Since we're talking about dogs and eating and bad stuff that can happen, let me add a note here on bloat. Bigger dogs tend to get this more than little ones, and 80% of them die when they do. I had a dog bloat and fortunately, we caught it as it was happening and a surgeon happened to be in the vet ER at 2am. She spent 3 days in intensive care and it cost us about $10,000. So worth it, but still.

Some dogs just develop this (like mine), but others seem to get it if they eat a huge amount, like if they find a bunch of food in the trash and gorge on it. You can recognize the symptoms because they will try to vomit but nothing will come up and their abdomen expands and gets really tight. My dog also started trying to find dark places to curl up and die – I still cry thinking about how scary that was. If your dog shows any of those symptoms, even a little, call your emergency vet ASAP and run every red light to get them there as fast as you can. The only chance you have to save them is getting them into surgery as fast as possible.

Thanks to all of you for reading, and may you and your pooches have many happy meals together!

Lightning Source UK Ltd.
Milton Keynes UK
UKHW050830020121
376110UK00002B/22